I Feel Good

Written by Susan Frame

Collins

I feel good in a gust of fresh air.

I hear twigs snap in the wind.

I feel good when I camp in a tent in the rain.

I let raindrops drip into my cup.

I feel good when I tramp up
the dust track.

I hear my feet crunch and scrunch.

I feel good when I swing on the swings.

I am a rocket. I swish up high.

I feel good when I do handstands.

I can feel the soft carpet under my hands.

I sit, think and drift. I feel good.

What things help you to feel good?

What helps you to feel good?

After reading

Letters and Sounds: Phase 4

Word count: 100

Focus on adjacent consonants with short vowel phonemes, e.g. *tent*.

Common exception words: I, of, the, when, my, do, what, you, to

Curriculum links: Personal, social and emotional development; Understanding the world

Curriculum links (National Curriculum, Year 1): Science; Human and physical geography; PSHE

Early learning goals: Reading: read and understand simple sentences; use phonic knowledge to decode regular words and read them aloud accurately; read some common irregular words

National Curriculum learning objectives: Reading/word reading: read accurately by blending sounds in unfamiliar words containing GPCs that have been taught; read other words of more than one syllable that contain taught GPCs; Reading/comprehension: develop pleasure in reading, motivation to read, vocabulary and understanding by being encouraged to link what they read or hear to their own experiences

Developing fluency

- Encourage your child to follow the words as you read the first pages with expression, asking your child to make sure you are reading words correctly.
- Take turns to read a double page, encouraging your child to use a different voice as if they are the child in each photograph.

Phonic practice

- Encourage your child to sound out and blend the following:

  snap   wind   tramp   crunch   swings   hands

- Focus on double syllable words. Check your child includes all the sounds, for example check they do not miss the middle "d" in **handstands**.

  raindrops   rocket   handstands   carpet

Extending vocabulary

- Challenge your child to think of a word with a similar meaning to the following.

  page 2: **fresh** (e.g. *cool, clean*) page 5: **drip** (e.g. *ping, drop*) page 9: **swish** (e.g. *fly, zoom*)

- Can your child think of a word that could be used instead of **good** for each page in the book? (e.g. *calm, free, happy, peaceful, excited*)